Peepshow

Written by Isabel Wright
Devised by Frantic Assembly

First performance of this production
Friday 20 September 2002

DRUM THEATRE PLYMOUTH
ROYAL PARADE | PLYMOUTH | PLI 2TR

LYRIC HAMMERSMITH   LONDON ARTS

Barclays Stage Partners

Peepshow

Autumn Tour Schedule 2002

20 September – 5 October
Drum Theatre Plymouth

8 – 12 October
Contact, Manchester

15 – 19 October
Gardner Arts Centre, Brighton

21 – 23 October
Theatre Royal Winchester

25 – 26 October
New Wolsey Theatre, Ipswich

29 October – 2 November
West Yorkshire Playhouse, Leeds

6 – 23 November
Lyric Hammersmith, London

Frantic has received in kind support from:

Peepshow

Cast

Kate Alderton	**Kate**
Sarah Beard	**Sarah**
Richard Dempsey	**Richard (Loner)**
Sharon Duncan-Brewster	**Sharon**
Ben Joiner	**Ben**
Georgina Lamb	**George**
Richard Mylan	**Richard**
Ingeborga Dapkunaite	Lithuanian Voice Over

Written by	Isabel Wright
Devised by	Frantic Assembly
Directors	Scott Graham
	Steven Hoggett
Songs and Creative Involvement	Andy Barlow
	Louise Rhodes (Lamb)
Choreographer	Dan O Neill
Design	Dick Bird
Lighting Design	Natasha Chivers
Musical Supervisor	Nicholas Skilbeck
Script Development	Lucy Morrison
	Literary Manager for Paines Plough
Production Manager	Jai Lusser
Company Stage Manager / Video Artist	Jeremy Nicholls
Sound Engineer	Marcus Wadland
Re-lights & LX Operator	Michelle Green
Technical ASM	Nick Shaw
Production Runner	Jenny Maddox
Set Build	Plymouth Theatre Royal Workshop
Drum Theatre Plymouth:	
Production Manager	Nick Soper
Wardrobe Supervisor	Dina Hall
Producer / Administrative Director	Vicki Coles
PR / Company Associate	Ben Chamberlain, Chamberlain McAuley
Graphic Design	Emma Cooke, Chamberlain McAuley
Education Coordinator	Sarah Quelch
Marketing Manager	Clair Chamberlain, Chamberlain McAuley

Biographies

Kate Alderton

Kate trained at LAMDA in London. Kate's credits include *Charley's Aunt* (Sheffield Crucible), Geraldine in Theatre Royal Bath's touring production of *What the Butler Saw* (dir. Jeremy Sams), *The Tempest* (ATC), *Powder Keg* (The Gate), *The Warp* (Ken Campbell) and *The Boy Who Left Home* (dir. Nick Phillipou). TV credits include *Doctors* (BBC), *The Bill* (Carlton) and *Noah's Ark 1 & 2* (Carlton). Film credits include *The Brother Present* (Paranoid Films) and *Fierce Creatures* (Fish Productions).

Sarah Beard

Sarah trained at Manchester Metropolitan University. She has worked extensively with Frantic Assembly on both national and international productions including *Service Charge* (Lyric Hammersmith), *Vs* (Co production with Karim Tonsy, Egypt), *Underworld* (national / international tour) and *Tiny Dynamite* (British Challenge Festival, Lithuania). Recent theatre includes *As You Like It* (Chapman), *Gulliver's Travels* (Walk The Plank), *Cover Up* (Action Transport Theatre Company), *Chameleon* (Sheffield Crucible), *Creaking Shadows* (Trading Faces) and most recently *The Grateful Servant* (Globe). As a dancer Sarah was involved in the Choreodrome season at The Place. Film and TV credits include *Rhinoceros* (Granada), *Seeing Red* (Granada), *Linda Green* (Red Productions), *At Home with the Braithwaites* (YTV) and *Mother's Day* (dir. Steen Argo and Howard Smith, Volt Films).

Richard Dempsey

Richard trained at Guildhall. Theatre credits include Flute in *A Midsummer Night's Dream* (RSC), Ugly in *Honk* (Stephen Joseph Theatre, Scarborough / National Theatre UK tour), Peter in *The Lion The Witch and The Wardrobe* (RSC), Nick in *Fame* (original West End cast), Jack in *Into The Woods* (original West End cast), Johnston in *Dance of Death* (Tricycle), Sam in *Gym and Tonic* (Theatre Royal, Windsor), *Lost Musicals* (Barbican and Fortune Theatre). TV credits include *The Real Antony and Cleopatra, The Ancients, Aristocrats, The Scarlet Pimpernel, Crime Traveller, Wings of Angels, Wives and Daughters, The Student Prince, Tilly Trotter, Sherlock Holmes, Don't Leave Me This Way, Good Guys, Inspector Allyn, Wycliffe, Red Peppers, Hands Across The Sea* and *The Chronicles of Narnia*. Film credits include *The Barber of Siberia, 24 Hours in London* and *The Prince of Jutland / Royal Deceit*. In addition Richard has recorded *Into The Woods, Fame* and *Honk*.

Sharon Duncan-Brewster

Sharon trained at Anna Sher Theatre School. Theatre credits include *Keepers* (Hampstead Theatre), *So Special* (Royal Exchange, Manchester), *Crave* (Paines Plough), *Yard Gal* (MCC Theatre on Broadway and Clean Break/Royal Court Theatre), *No Boys Cricket Club* (Theatre Royal, Stratford East) plus *Ashes and Sand* and *Babies* (Royal Court Theatre Upstairs). Film credits include *Body Story* (Redstar) and *Christmas* (Ch4./World Pictures). TV credits include *The Bill, Casualty, Hope I Die Before I Get*

Old, Between the Lines and *2.4 Children* (BBC). She has just completed her role of Crystal in her fourth series of *Bad Girls* (Granada) and is about to reprise the role of Evelyn in the second series of *Babyfather* (BBC2).

Ben Joiner

Ben trained at The Welsh College of Music and Drama and the Northern School of Contemporary Dance. Theatre credits include *Laurent in Thérese Raquin* (WCMD), *Tell Me* (Northern Stage at the Donmar Warehouse), *Without Trace* (V Tol Dance Company at The Southbank), *Hard Shoulder* (Retina Dance Company - national / international tour), and *Rhino* (Dodgy Clutch Theatre Company - national tour). Film credits include The Search and Pink (CYFLE / WCMD Production - Producer Pennant Roberts).

Georgina Lamb

Georgina trained at Manchester Metropolitan University. Theatre credits include *Unsuitable Girls* (Pilot Theatre Company, Leicester Haymarket), *Beyond the Wall and Over the Sea* and *Death of a Salesman* (both for Leicester Haymarket) and *Beauty and the Beast* (Library Theatre, Manchester). For Frantic Assembly *Underworld* (Lyric Hammersmith and national tour), *Zero* and *Klub* (BAC, national and international tours). For Trestle Theatre Company *Hanging Around*, *The Barratts of Wimpole Street*, *Island* and *Bitter Fruit*. Additional credits include *Fascinations from the Crowd* (Fecund Theatre, BAC and national tour), Three's a Crowd (Milca Leon Dance Company, The Place), *Cushioned Souls* (Pleasance, Edinburgh) and *Die Meistersinger Von Nuremberg*

(Royal Opera House). Film credits include *The Last Train* (Ascalon Films/Whatever Pictures).

Richard Mylan

Richard trained at Urdang Academy of Performing Arts. Theatre credits include *Crazy Gary's Mobile Disco* (Paines Plough, national tour), *Badfinger* (Donmar Warehouse) and *Starlight Express*. Richard is currently working on the new Dawn French project, *Wild West* (dir. Jonathan Gershfield) and has just finished filming on *A&E* (dir. Chris King) which follows filming on his second series of *Belonging* (BBC Wales). Other TV credits include *Silent Witness*, *Border Café*, Score and *Casualty* (all BBC). He also recently returned to *The Bill* for his third 3 hour story playing the drugs dealer Leroy Jones.

Isabel Wright Writer

Isabel studied Drama at the Royal Scottish Academy of Music and Drama. Previous plays include *Speedrun* (dir. Irina Brown, Tron Theatre), *Waiting Room* (Complete Productions, dir. Gordon Laird, Tron Theatre), *Tongues* (Lookout Theatre, dir. Nicole McCartney, Scottish tour), *Blooded* (Boilerhouse, dir. Paul Pinson, Scottish tour) and *Initiate* (Boilerhouse Education). She was Writer in Residence at the Traverse Theatre in 2001 and is currently Writer in Residence at the Bush Theatre. Isabel has been commissioned by the Traverse to write two plays, and she is also writing one for the Bush Theatre.

Scott Graham Director

Scott co-founded Frantic Assembly in 1994 and is Artistic Director with the company. He has performed in and co-directed Frantic productions including *Look Back In Anger, The Generation Trilogy: Klub, Flesh* and *Zero, Sell Out, Hymns* and *Tiny Dynamite* (collaboration with Paines Plough). He co-directed Frantic's *Underworld* and *Service Charge* (Lyric Hammersmith). Scott appeared in *Outside Now* for Prada (Milan Fashion Week 2000) and directed *Air* for MAC's Blue Zone and *Frantic for TLC* for JWT Advertising. Scott also co-directed and devised *Vs*, a co-production with Egyptian based Karim Tonsy Dance Company for the Cairo International Festival of Experimental Theatre.

Steven Hoggett Director

Steven is Co-founder and Artistic Director of Frantic Assembly. Director / performer credits for Frantic: *Look Back In Anger, The Generation Trilogy: Klub, Flesh* and *Zero, Sell Out, Hymns, Vs* (collaboration with Karim Tonsy Dance Company, Cairo Festival) and *Tiny Dynamite* (collaboration with Paines Plough). Frantic directorial work includes *Service Charge* for the Lyric Hammersmith, *Frantic for TLC* for JWT Advertising and *Air* for MAC's Blue Zone and *Underworld*. Additional choreography for Oily Cart, Wink Productions and if performance collective. Additional performance work includes *Manifesto* for Volcano Theatre Company, *Go Las Vegas* for The Featherstonehaughs and *Outside Now* for Prada (Milan Fashion Week 2000).

Dick Bird Designer

Dick Bird's recent designs include *Monkey!* At the Young Vic, *A Prayer for Owen Meany* and *The Walls* for the Royal National Theatre, *The Lady in the Van* for West Yorkshire Playhouse, *My Fair Lady* and *Closer* for Teatro El Nacional, Buenos Aires, *Il Tabarro* and *Vollo do Notte* for Long Beach Opera in California, *Light* for Theatre de Complicite and *The Three Musketeers* (dir. Julian Weber) for the Young Vic. He has worked extensively with Primitive Science including *Vagabondage, Icarus Falling, Poseidon* and most recently *The Invisible College* at the Salzburg Festival. Previously for Frantic Assembly *Heavenly*.

Natasha Chivers
Lighting Designer

Recent theatre work includes *After The Dance* for Oxford Stage company (national tour), *The Drowned World* for Paines Plough (Traverse Theatre, Edinburgh), *Chaste Maid in Cheapside* (Almeida Theatre Company), *Helmet* (Traverse Theatre / Paines Plough tour), *Tiny Dynamite* (Frantic Assembly/Paines Plough/Contact Theatre tour), *1001 Nights* and *The Firebird* for Unicorn Theatre Company, *Life with An Idiot* (The Gate Theatre, London), *Among Unbroken Hearts* (Traverse Theatre tour and Bush Theatre), *Crazy Gary's Mobile Disco* (Paines Plough / Sgript Cymru tour), *A Listening Heaven* (Royal Lyceum Theatre, Edinburgh), *Eliza's House* (Royal Exchange Theatre, Manchester), *Notre Dame de Paris* (Strathcona Theatre Company tour), *Sweet Phoebe* by Michael Gow (2002 Sydney Festival), *Hymns* and *Sell Out* for Frantic Assembly and *Buried Alive* (tour) and *Demons and Dybbuks* (Young Vic) for Method and Madness. Natasha has also designed lighting for numerous site-specific works throughout the UK.

Dan O Neill Choreographer

Dan has choreographed for film, TV (BBC, Channel 4, Canal+), the theatre (Young Vic, The Place, Royal National Theatre, ICA, Royal Lyceum) and the commercial sector. He was Choreographer and Associate Director on the Young Vic's *Monkey!*. He also choreographed the Unicorn Theatre's *Red Red Shoes* which began its national tour at Royal Opera House's Linbury Studio earlier this year. In the commercial sector Dan worked on *Jesus Christ Superstar* and *Dr Doolittle* in London, *Honk* in Scarborough and *Rent* in Finland. Dan wrote and choreographed *The Linesman*, commissioned by the Arts Council/BBC/NPS. Initially broadcast in England on BBC2 and in Holland in NPS, it has been screened at international film festivals including London, Paris, New York and Rio. He has directed and choreographed several other films including the award-winning *Struck, Howdy Doody* and *Lapse*, which is currently touring as part of the Capture programme. Dan has recently completed another short film, *Tag*.

Nicholas Skilbeck
Musical Supervisor

Nicholas Skilbeck graduated from the Royal Academy of Music in 1998. He started his career at Oldham Coliseum as musical director and arranger for a production of Pam Gems's *Piaf*. Since then he worked in an impro comedy troupe, improvised silent film scores, even had a spell as Musical Director of the Casino, Monte Carlo. Since 1994 Nicholas has worked closely with performer/writer Nigel Charnock, and spent several years touring with him, composing the scores, co-writing songs and being the musician on stage, with their most recent collaboration being *Asylum* (Queen Elizabeth Hall and national tour). Nicholas is the co-author of *The Singing and Acting Handbook: Games and Exercises for the Performer* (published by Routledge) which is used as a text book at universities and performing arts institutions in the UK and USA . Recent work as Musical Director includes Victoria Wood's *At It Again* (Royal Albert Hall and broadcast on ITV 2002). He is currently Assistant Musical Director of *Chitty Chitty Bang Bang* (London Palladium). Nicholas is going to be a father for the second time in October and already has a beautiful daughter called Eden.

Jai Lusser
Production Manager

Previous Production Manager credits include *Heavenly* for Frantic Assembly, *Stomp* (European and Far East tour), *A House of Correction* for The Wrestling School, *The Magic Flute* for Garden Opera, *Maps of Desire* for Wonderful Beast and *BOING!* for Oily Cart. He has also worked as Production Manager for The Pleasance in Edinburgh as part of a working relationship spanning 5 years. Jai has worked regularly with The Wrestling School including the 8-hour epic *The Ecstatic Bible* (Adelaide Festival) and English Touring Theatre including *The York Realist* (Royal Court and West End). Other credits include *Baddiel and Skinner Unplanned*, *Lulu* (Almeida King's Cross), *Ennio Marchetto*, *Saucy Jack and the Space Vixens*, *The Oxygen Project*, Fecund Theatre and Mel and Sue.

Jeremy Nicholls Company Stage Manager / Video Artist

Jeremy trained at Theatre in the Mill, Bradford. Since then he has worked for Phoenix Arts in Leicester, Open Hand Theatre Company, and as Production Manager for Alhambra Studio and Twisting Yarn Theatre Company in Bradford, working in partnership with Chol Theatre, Bradford Festival and Opera North. Jeremy has also worked as a set designer for Twisting Yarn Theatre Company, for the Oldham Coliseum and Peshkar as Production Manager and Set Designer for *The Beautiful Violin*; as designer for Theatre in the Mill's New Writing Festival 2002 and has worked with Frantic since 2001, touring *Underworld, Tiny Dynamite* (a co-production with Paines Plough) *and Heavenly* as Company Stage Manager and Video Artist.

Marcus Wadland
Sound Engineer

Recent work includes a year as sound engineer on *Joseph and the Amazing Technicolor Dreamcoat* ongoing UK tour, *Leader of the Pack* UK tour, Sound Operator *Brief Encounter* at the Lyric Shaftsbury Avenue, acting deputy chief electrician at the Young Vic Theatre, touring sound engineer Method and Madness, shows included *Demons and Dybbuks, The Black Dahlia, The Cherry Orchard* and the world premiere of Philip Osment's *Buried Alive*. Other work includes technician at the Barbican Centre, London, electrician at Derby Playhouse and the Bradford Alhambra. Work on Frantic shows

Hymns, Sell Out and *Tiny Dynamite* (a co-production with Paines Plough) in Lithuania. Electrician on festivals, conferences and concerts throughout the UK and sound engineer for Orbital sound company.

Michelle Green
Re-lights & LX Operator

Relights include *The Noise of Time* USA and European tours for Theatre de Complicite, *Shoot to Win* UK tour for Theatre Royal Stratford East, *Under Your Hat* for Oily Cart at the Lyric Hammersmith and Paris, *Some Explicit Polaroids* UK tour for Out of Joint. Lighting design includes rehearsed readings series at the Royal Court Theatre Upstairs, *In The Face of a Stranger* and *Plastic Chill* for First Person Dance Company and After Liverpool for Play Club Production Company.

Nick Shaw TASM

Nick trained at Central School of Speech and Drama. Credits include Cannizaro Park Open Air Theatre Season, TSM *for In the Solitude of Cotton Fields* Actor's Touring Company, TASM for *Bewildrness* UK tour for The Right Size, stage technician for *Mamma Mia* at the Prince Edward Theatre and *Show Boat* at the Prince Edward Theatre and Pleasance Two, stage technician and flyman at Pleasance One, stage manager and technician for *I Am A Coffee* for Peepolykus and head flyman for *Amadeus* at the Old Vic, TSM and acting deputy TSM for Lyric Hammersmith and TSM for *Swan Song* at the Pleasance London.

"It's about trusting everything to flow." (lamb)

Lamb are Lou Rhodes and Andy Barlow.

Lamb have created some of the most innovative sounds and moods of the 21st century, communicated some of the most touching lyrics, and in six years have written three groundbreaking albums - the eponymously titled album in 1996, the second **Fear of Fours** in 1999 and in 2002 the highly acclaimed **What Sound**. Their high emotional charge, haunting vocals and intense beat-driven songs have established a genre-bending mixture of drum and bass, hip-hop, techno, blues, classical and jazz.

What Sound reflects Andy and Lou at their most relaxed; open and energised, with freshly charged expression of all that is characteristically Lamb. The album features various guest musicians, including Jimi Goodwin from Doves, Michael Franti, Me'Shell NdegeOcello, Scratch Perverts, Wil Malone and Arto Lindsay.

This year has also seen the re-emergence of one of Lamb's most powerful songs, **Gorecki**, on the Baz Lurman film **Moulin Rouge**.

Lou Rhodes and Andy Barlow are now working with the groundbreaking theatre company Frantic Assembly to produce a soundtrack for the lives of the characters that appear in the moving production of **Peepshow**.

You can see them live on tour with Moby throughout November.

www.lambstar.net

For more information please call
Sarah Pearson on 020 7453 4463.

franticassembly

Frantic Assembly was founded in 1994 by Artistic Directors Scott Graham and Steven Hoggett and Administrative Director Vicki Coles.

'**No company working in Britain today has done so much to make theatre accessible and relevant to a generation of twenty-somethings**' *Big Issue*

Renowned both nationally and internationally for attracting new, young, audiences, Frantic Assembly stand at the forefront of new British physical theatre. In just eight years, Frantic has established itself as one of the most innovative and exciting companies around, touring extensively throughout the UK including a pioneering West End run in 1999. Six time recipients of Time Out Critic's Choice, the company also received a Time Out Live award for Sell Out in 1998. To date, Frantic have presented their work in over 20 different countries over 4 continents and are now studied at GCSE, 'A' and Degree level throughout Britain.

Frantic's work has been described as 'the bleeding edge of contemporary British Theatre' (*The Stage*), 'Theatre of the 21st Century' (*Guardian*), 'Crucial viewing for anyone interested in the future of theatre (*Time Out*).

'**They have created a piece of theatre that, on the ladder of excellence, is only a few rungs short from sheer theatrical nirvana**' *What's On*

Following huge success with **Look Back In Anger** (94), **Klub** (95), **Flesh** (96) and **Zero** (97), Frantic's recent credits include award-winning **Sell Out** (98), **Hymns** (99), **Underworld** (01), **Tiny Dynamite** – a Co-Production with Paines Plough and Contact, Manchester (01) and **Heavenly** (02). Since April 02, Frantic has been in receipt of Fixed Term Funding from London Arts.

Frantic Assembly
BAC, Lavender Hill
London SW11 5TF
Tel / Fax 020 7228 8885
Email: vicki@franticassembly.co.uk
www.franticassembly.co.uk

The Resource Pack: A Teacher's Comprehensive Guide to Peepshow is available free to schools. Please contact Vicki Coles for more details.

Sell Out 1998   Hymns 1999   Underworld 2000   Tiny Dynamite 2001   Heavenly 2002

CO-PRODUCER FOR
Peepshow

A LONDON ORIGINAL

Photo: Steve Tanner

Photo: Erick Labbe

Photo: Richard Haughton

Photo: Paul Miller

Kneehigh Theatre	Ex-Machina	Lyric Hammersmith	Pilot Theatre
THE RED SHOES	**LA CASA AZUL**	**A CHRISTMAS CAROL**	**ROAD**
18 Sep–5 Oct	11–26 Oct	29 Nov–4 Jan	15 Jan–1 Feb

MAKING NEW THEATRE; MAKING THEATRE NEW

Hidden away behind a concrete façade on a busy high street, the Lyric has always been one of the most surprising theatres in London.

Over the next eight months the Lyric Hammersmith consolidates its position as one of London's most original producing theatres with a season of work from the best of the new generation of theatre makers – cutting edge companies such as Kneehigh, Pilot, Improbable and Northern Stage, working alongside directors like Robert Lepage, Neil Bartlett and David McVicar. I am especially delighted that we have been able to work with Frantic Assembly again, making this new production *Peepshow* together as a major part of our current season.

While all of this is happening on our stages, we are also busy developing plans with architect Rick Mather for a dramatic new glass-fronted entrance sweeping down into the Lyric Square, a new ticket office and café, and, behind the scene, two new spaces – a purpose built rehearsal space and a dedicated education room.

Meantime, some things never change at the Lyric; free first nights, great value tickets, bargain Mondays and an audience as varied as the city we live and work in. The doors of this theatre, I'm proud to say, are wide open. I hope you'll visit us when you're next in London.

Neil Bartlett, Artistic Director

020 8741 2311, www.lyric.co.uk

Registered Charity No 278518

THEATRE ROYAL PLYMOUTH

The Theatre Royal Plymouth opened in 1982 and in just 20 years has built up a reputation as one of the largest and best attended regional theatres in the UK.

The Theatre Royal Plymouth regularly produces or co-produces some of the biggest and most innovative work in the country. Musical successes which have transferred to the West End include **Buddy, Fame, Jolson, Spend Spend Spend** and **Peggy Sue Got Married**.

Recent drama collaborations include Ben Elton's **Inconceivable** (with West Yorkshire Playhouse), **Tender** (with Birmingham Rep & Hampstead Theatre) and **Hobson's Choice** (with Birmingham Rep & The Touring Partnership).

As well as **Peepshow**, Autumn 2002 sees the Theatre Royal Plymouth co-producing Edward Woodward in **Goodbye Gilbert Harding** (with the New Vic) and Richard Briers in **The Tempest** (with Thelma Holt). In the Drum the Theatre Royal Plymouth's Artistic Director Simon Stokes will direct **The Green Man** by Doug Lucie.

Also this year the Theatre Royal Plymouth is opening a purpose-built Production & Education Centre in Plymouth, providing unrivalled creative, construction and rehearsal facilities for its productions as well as a cultural resource for the people of the South West.

www.theatreroyal.com

Chief Executive **Adrian Vinken**
Artistic Director **Simon Stokes**
General Manager **Alan Finch**
Technical Director **Ed Wilson**

THEATRE ROYAL PLYMOUTH

is a registered charity no. 284545
& gratefully receives funding from

GOODBYE GILBERT HARDING

PEEPSHOW

THE TEMPEST

THE GREEN MAN

Directors' Note

A Frantic show with songs first began as an idea after a performance of **Hymns** in London in 1999. After the performance an audience member explained how she had expected two characters to sing at the end of a particular scene. The realisation that this didn't seem at all ludicrous to us was the start of the **Peepshow** project.

After seeing such work as Massive Attack's video for **Protection**, the use of Aimee Mann's songs in the film **Magnolia** and Zero 7's track **Destiny**, we decided to look at ways in which we might create a Frantic theatre piece which added live singing into the mix. Our use of music to soundtrack in previous work and our blatant visual and structural theft from the music video genre meant that songs being presented theatrically was really more of a natural progression for the company. Once our Co-Producers the Drum Theatre Plymouth and the Lyric Hammersmith were on board, the project could start to move forward.

An initial idea was to use songs by a variety of artists, but we realised pretty quickly that the range and feeling we required for the entire piece existed within one unique back catalogue. The Lamb sound has been with us since their debut in 1996, serving as a constant inspiration in our rehearsal rooms over the years. What started out as a company dream became a possibility when after months of empty wishing, procrastination and hiding, our dearest Manchester angel, Liam Walsh, passed across a telephone receiver telling us the Lamb manager was about to pick up at the other end. Twenty minutes later we had definite interest. A second call two weeks later resulted in a pencilled yes. A confirmed yes the following month rendered Gordon Biggins the title of Most Beautiful Manager Ever To Grace The Music Business With His Truly Divine Presence. Our first meeting with Lou and Andy was nerve racking for the simple reason that, at this point, all we had to offer was a concept. Something about our sweaty palms and our occasionally squeaky voices must have appealed to both of them. Their generosity and trust since then has made this working relationship a true privilege.

The scale of the piece is a conscious departure from previous work. **Peepshow** offers us a chance to explore tiny truths, moments and details but on an expanded scale – one that allows us to play with notions of contrast and comparison as well as our usual ingredients, intimacy and intensity. In taking this significant step up in scale, it was essential for us to find our strongest creative team yet. Luckily, we did find them, and in Isabel, Dan, Dick, Natasha, Jai, Jez, Nicholas, Marcus, Lucy and Jenny we have found practitioners with an incredible ability to both recognise and share a vision at a very early stage. Collectively, they are a formidable, fearless and visionary group of people whose skills and support were and are a constant source of excitement to work with.

The nature of the show posed a huge challenge in terms of performers. Auditions for the show were the most difficult and extensive ever undertaken by the company. In addition to doing that Frantic thing in terms of both movement skills and understanding of text, auditionees also had the huge task of getting to grips with the Lamb sound and then presenting that in an audition room. Before we held the auditions, we weren't even sure that such performers were out there. Today we're almost half way through rehearsals and there are lots of things we have yet to discover, but the versatility and bravery of our cast has already given us a sense of confidence we never thought possible at this stage. With over three weeks still left, this feels like an incredibly rich and exciting time for Frantic Assembly. Our hope is that the end result will reflect this.

Scott Graham and Steven Hoggett
27 August 2002

Thanks to:

Matt Berry at The Almeida, Stuart Griffiths, Nick Middleton, Marco Favarro, Nigel Charnock, Simon Stokes and all at Theatre Royal Plymouth, Simon Mellor and all at Lyric Hammersmith, Adam Stanley, Cliff Wilding, Michael Wynne, Laurie Sansom, Gwilym Morris, Karen Gillingham and David Lamb. In addition Richard Mylan would like to thank Catrin and Ella.

Extra special thanks for deeds above and beyond the call of duty: Sian Teasdale, Gordon Biggins, Paines Plough, John Tiffany, Liam Walsh and Isabel Wright.

Barclays Stage Partners

For more than six years, Barclays Stage Partners has been creating unique, and sometimes unusual opportunities for audiences of all age groups throughout the UK to see top quality theatre.

Bringing theatre to a wider audience

The scheme has supported 64 productions, touring to over 160 theatres across the UK, reaching an audience approaching 2 million.

This autumn, Barclays Stage Partners, with the Arts Council of England, is supporting tours by *Be My Baby, A Passage to India, Peepshow* and *A View from the Bridge*.

Barclays Stage Partners is an integral part of Barclays overall community investment programme. Barclays global contribution to community causes totalled £31.1 million in 2001, which includes their commitment to contribute 1% of UK pre-tax profits to community investment, making Barclays one of the UK's largest corporate contributors and the third largest worldwide. Barclays supports five main areas – education, the disadvantaged, social inclusion, the arts and the environment. The aim of the Barclays community programme is to achieve real and lasting benefit both for the community and Barclays.

Over the next two years, Barclays commitment to the arts will continue with *Invest and Inspire*, a £1.9 million commitment to promote wider public access to the arts, involving the Royal National Theatre, The British Museum, The National Gallery and Tate Britain.

For details about Barclays Stage Partners call 020 7221 7883.

BARCLAYS

PEEPSHOW

Running Order 27/8/02

Gorecki

Five: Clothy / Unpack / Chips /
        Gift / Vampire / Ben
        Visit / Shitty / Spesk

Loner Hang

Wine

Yo Pimpin Ass

Zero

Mr. Ripley

Soft Mistake

How Do I ...

Funny Fish

Box

Lift Life

Lithuanian Photos / Rabbit

Milch Cow

Bonfire

He'd Like Your Laugh

Feela

Werewolves

Pewk

Me or Him

Lithuanian Flirt

Walkman

Creepy / Pervy

Levi

Gabriel

One: George? / Jealous / Invisible /
      Don't Leave Me / Hello /
      [Lift] / I Love You /
      Princess / You're Scared ...

Cocky Del Boy

Last Word

Rocket

Just Is

Connect

First published in 2002 by Oberon Books Ltd.
(incorporating Absolute Classics)
521 Caledonian Road, London N7 9RH
Tel: 020 7607 3637 / Fax: 020 7607 3629
e-mail: oberon.books@btinternet.com
www.oberonbooks.com

A catalogue record for this book is available from the British
Library.

ISBN: 1 84002 345 7

Cover design: Emma Cooke, Chamberlain McAuley

Printed in Great Britain by Antony Rowe Ltd, Chippenham.

Characters

RICHARD

SHARON

BEN

GEORGE

LONER

SARAH

KATE

A cross section of the rooms of a towerblock: the show cuts quickly from room to room; the action can therefore be seen in more than one room simultaneously.

Physical trailer for the show, over 'Gorecki'. Collage of images that are to follow.

'Five' plays under the following scenes.

One

In blackout, heard by other characters. Reactions of other characters.

GEORGE: No! Get off me! Get off me!

BEN: George.

GEORGE: You're hurting me! Stop it! Get off!

BEN: Keep your voice down.

GEORGE: I'll fucking shout if I want to. You drag me around. You push me about.

BEN: I'm not pushing you.

GEORGE: Stop it!

BEN: Stop what?

> *Lights come up on BEN and GEORGE. She is drunkenly stumbling around with one heel of her shoe broken. BEN is trying to hold her up, is laughing at her.*

GEORGE: Stop it.

BEN: What?

GEORGE: That thing with your face.

BEN: I'm doing nothing with my face.

GEORGE: You know what you're doing. You do it to drive me mad.

GEORGE stumbles.

BEN: Careful.

GEORGE: Am fine.

BEN: Don't want to fall now do you?

GEORGE: Am fine. Fine. Fine. Fine.

BEN: Come to bed.

GEORGE: No! The night is young.

BEN: Come to bed.

GEORGE: I didn't want to come home.

BEN: Nobody made you.

GEORGE: You made me!

BEN: I didn't.

GEORGE: So I'm to come home alone. Raped, slashed, murdered to pieces on the tube?

BEN: Murdered to pieces?

GEORGE: You'd like that. You'd like to see me dead. You'd say, serves you right.

BEN: And why on earth would I say that?

GEORGE: Because you're boring and you won't let me drink.

BEN: You were humiliating yourself.

GEORGE: I brought the party to life.

BEN: You embarassed everyone.

GEORGE: One little smeggy table lamp.

BEN: It was their wedding present.

GEORGE: It was…vile. Crying out to be broken.

BEN: You're too fucking much

GEORGE: You. Are too fucking little. I bring you to life.

BEN: You bring me to my knees.

GEORGE: Yeah, you fucking love it.

TWO

SARAH is moving into KATE's flat.

KATE: Is that everything?

SARAH: I think so.

KATE: Gonna be great isn't it?

SARAH: I know it seems a lot.

KATE: No it's… It's…fine.

SARAH: Do you get much light in here?

KATE: It's lovely on Sunday mornings. Having breakfast in the sunlight. It's gonna be a right laugh.

SARAH: Give me the tour then.

KATE: Well the shower doesn't work.

SARAH: In what way doesn't work.

KATE: It blasts out hot and cold randomly and then gives up the ghost.

SARAH: I'll take a look at it.

KATE: Could you?

SARAH: Can I sleep by the window?

KATE: Yes – I mean – I can move.

SARAH: Would you? I won't sleep otherwise.

KATE: No, that's – okay.

SARAH: This could be the best room ever.

KATE: Yeah.

SARAH: Just needs a bit of…

KATE: The phone has that call waiting thingy – but I haven't got it figured out yet.

SARAH: Kate, it's easy.

KATE: I'm no good at all that.

SARAH: I'll take a look at it.

KATE: Gonna be a right laugh this. Our own boudoir.

SARAH: Our own den of sin! Girls' gang hut.

KATE: Our own place.

SARAH: You got any house rules for me?

KATE: Em. I don't think so.

SARAH: Well I've got a few ideas. Just to keep things tidy. Ticking over.

KATE: Okay.

SARAH: It's gonna be brilliant.

KATE: Yeah.

Three

GEORGE and BEN.

GEORGE: I didn't want to come home.

BEN: Nobody made you.

GEORGE: (*Mimicking.*) Nobody made you.

BEN: The party was over.

GEORGE: Was hardly bloody starting.

BEN: Jennifer said she wanted something quiet.

GEORGE: Ooh Jennifer Smennifer… She needs a personality bypass.

BEN: (*Laughing.*) George! You never listen! Never care what anyone else is thinking!

GEORGE: I do care!

BEN: Sometimes it's good to sense when it's time to leave.

GEORGE: They wanted you to leave. You destroyed the party! Sucked the life from it! You're a bloody party black hole!

BEN: You're a bloody lush.

GEORGE: You're a bloody wet blanket.

BEN: You're a bloody nuisance.

GEORGE: People want me there. I'm entertaining.

BEN: Like watching a car crash. Go to sleep George.

GEORGE: Why?

BEN: Because.

GEORGE: Maybe I'll stay up all night.

BEN: And sleep all tomorrow?

GEORGE: Can if I want.

Four

RICHARD and SHARON.

RICHARD enters.

RICHARD: Hey baby.

SHARON is listening to GEORGE and BEN's argument.

SHARON: Ssh.

Five

BEN and GEORGE.

BEN: Come to bed.

GEORGE: It's early. You're so boring. I want some wine.

BEN: No you don't.

GEORGE: Get me some.

BEN: George…

GEORGE: Get me some!

BEN: Keep your –

GEORGE: Get me some!

BEN: Keep your voice down.

GEORGE: I'm not a fucking child!

BEN: Okay.

GEORGE: I want some wine!

BEN: Okay. We'll have some wine. Just don't shout.

GEORGE: I'll shout all I fucking want. You hear me bastards?! Remember when we were in halls. That was life. That was something. This is like night of the living dead. You hear me zombies?!

BEN: Ssh, George. Ssh.

GEORGE: I won't go to sleep.

BEN: Okay.

GEORGE: I'm going to make some chips.

BEN: No you're not.

GEORGE: I am. Do you want some chips?

BEN: You're not making any chips.

GEORGE: Why not?

BEN: Because you'll set yourself alight.

GEORGE: Boring bastard. You're a boring bastard. You know that?

BEN: I am a boring bastard.

GEORGE: Just as long as you know.

BEN: Have some water.

GEORGE: No.

BEN: Have some water.

GEORGE: No!

BEN: Drink some bloody water!

> *GEORGE pours the water over BEN. For a moment she thinks he will be angry. Then they both laugh.*

You're too fucking much.

GEORGE: You're too fucking little.

Six

RICHARD and SHARON.

SHARON: Where've you been?

RICHARD: I'm only a bit late.

SHARON: I was worried.

RICHARD: I'm here now.

SHARON: I thought something had happened.

RICHARD: What would happen?

SHARON: I was worried you'd come off the bike again.

RICHARD: Don't need to worry about me. I'm invincible.

SHARON: I do worry about you.

RICHARD: I'm on a roll. In the zone. Cooking with gas. It's been an amazing night. Did you see the sky? Looked like it was on fire.

SHARON: What have you been doing?

RICHARD: This and that. You know. Doing the do.

SHARON: Talk properly to me.

RICHARD: Nothing. I haven't been doing anything. Riding around. You look nice.

SHARON shrugs.

What have you been doing?

SHARON: Nothing. Waiting for you.

RICHARD: You haven't been out?

SHARON: I've been waiting for you!

RICHARD: I'm sorry baby. I'm sorry. I've got something for you.

He crawls on the bed with his shoes on.

SHARON: Don't.

He takes his shoes off.

Just hold me.

He doesn't hear her.

RICHARD: Don't you want to see it? (*He gives her a necklace.*) You like it? You like it?

She almost cries.

You hate it.

SHARON: It's beautiful.

RICHARD: Put it on.

SHARON: No.

RICHARD: Put it on.

SHARON: No.

Pause.

So?

RICHARD: What?

SHARON: You know what.

RICHARD: I don't baby.

SHARON: Where did you get the money?

RICHARD: What money?

SHARON: To buy me gifts.

RICHARD: You hate it. It's just a gift. To make you feel nice. It's just a gift.

She decides to take the gift.

SHARON: You promise?

RICHARD: I saved. I promise.

He puts the necklace on her.

SHARON: Touch me.

He doesn't know how to touch her the way she wants to be touched.

Seven

KATE and SARAH.

SARAH finds KATE's red dress. It is brash and tarty.

SARAH: What the hell is this?

KATE: Don't.

SARAH: Is it yours?

KATE: It's…just for fun.

SARAH: You don't wear this do you?

KATE: Sometimes. For fun.

SARAH: Not really you is it?

KATE: Well. It can be me sometimes.

SARAH: Look a right slapper in that!

KATE: Just a bit of fun.

SARAH: Like I said. Not really you.

KATE: I have that side to me too, you know? I have my wild side.

SARAH: Yeah?

KATE: Most people don't see it, that's all.

SARAH: And how does this…wild side…manifest itself?

KATE: Well… You know.

SARAH: You re a bit of a vamp sometimes, that what you're saying?

KATE: I could be.

SARAH: Give it up Kate. It's me.

KATE: I can be fearless. Slutty. Liberated.

SARAH: Whatever you say.

KATE: I could!

SARAH: You're a big softie Kate and you know it. You want hearts and roses and Mills and Boon covers. I see the way you look at Jake.

KATE: What's Jake got to do with anything?

SARAH: I know how you feel about him.

KATE: I don't know what you mean. And I'm not a softie. My mind is tough. I could go down to the 'Pig and Firkin' and pick up any guy I fancied just for sex.

SARAH is laughing.

You just don't know what I'm capable of.

SARAH: Okay Kate I believe you. You tease people and use people and then you discard them. You could head out there tonight and sell your body to pay the rent.

KATE: I could. I could if I wanted.

SARAH: Oh Kate love.

KATE: And I don't fancy your brother.

SARAH: Okay. Whatever you say.

KATE: I don't.

SARAH: Fine. That's just a shame. Because I think he likes you.

KATE: Really?

SARAH: You do fancy him!

KATE: Well, maybe just a little.

SARAH: Maybe I could get you two together.

KATE: You think you could?

SARAH: Sure.

Pause.

KATE: It's gonna be great this.

SARAH: Yeah.

Eight

BEN is in RICHARD and SHARON's room.

SHARON is startled to see BEN in her room.

SHARON: Oh. Hello.

RICHARD: What was it you wanted again?

SHARON: Can I get you a drink?

BEN: Well. It's a bit stupid. But I wondered if I could borrow a bottle opener. We seem to have been a bit careless with ours.

SHARON: Of course.

BEN: You know how it is.

SHARON: No problem.

BEN: I'll bring it right back.

RICHARD: You live downstairs?

BEN: Yeah. (*Pause.*) You might have heard a bit of noise earlier.

RICHARD/SHARON: No, not at all.

BEN: There was a bit of – noise. Sorry.

SHARON: We didn't hear anything at all. Did we?

RICHARD: Everything's alright now?

BEN: Well. You know… Just a bit of silly shouting.

RICHARD: You should come round one night. You and your – girlfriend

BEN: That'd be good.

RICHARD: Or maybe you two can rendezvous in the lift again?

Pause.

BEN: Well thanks for this.

SHARON: We meant it. The dinner. It wasn't just something you say.

BEN: Yeah I know. Thanks.

Pause.

RICHARD: Was there anything else?

BEN: No. This is great. Listen. Sorry about the noise. George can be a bit – high-spirited.

SHARON: We honestly didn't hear anything.

RICHARD: As long as you weren't killing each other.

BEN: Nothing like that. Well. See you around.

SHARON: See you.

BEN leaves.

Cut to SARAH and KATE. SARAH is laughing hysterically, KATE is trying to understand the joke, isn't laughing as much.

RICHARD: He's a funny one isn't he?

SHARON: In what way?

RICHARD: I guess guys just notice these things about other guys.

SHARON: What exactly?

RICHARD: He's kind of shifty.

SHARON: That's rubbish.

RICHARD: How do you know?

SHARON: I don't.

RICHARD: I thought you didn't know him.

SHARON: I don't. What is this?

RICHARD: Then I might be right.

SHARON: He seems perfectly nice.

RICHARD: You think everyone's nice. You only see the best in people. I've heard them…

SHARON: Shagging?

RICHARD: No! Fighting. Sounds like he knocks her about.

SHARON: He doesn't look like the sort.

RICHARD: They never do. Have you heard them shagging?

SHARON: No.

RICHARD: I can just tell a shifty bloke when I see one.

SHARON: You'd know about that wouldn't you? With your colleagues. Business associates.

RICHARD: Just making an observation baby.

SHARON: A stupid one.

Pause.

He touches the necklace.

RICHARD: I didn't know if you'd want gold or silver.

SHARON: It's fine Richard. It's fine.

Pause.

Nine

BEN and GEORGE are sulking. Move warily round each other.

BEN: I'm not gonna be the first to speak.

GEORGE: Neither am I.

Ten

LONER with his anti-gravity boots. He has a mobile phone.

LONER: It's me.
You probably won't get this.
If you do, then, you know, call.
I was wondering if Bangkok was how you imagined it.
If your accent was improving.
Are you still in Bangkok?
Where are you now?
I was wondering if you were still thinking of staying on.
Just…
You said you might that's all.
My voice keeps echoing back at me. I sound like a lunatic.
I was wondering if you'd decided to stay in that mad old hotel.

The one you said looked like it was run by trolls.
I was wondering…
Well.
Call me anyway.
If you're busy that's okay.
I miss you.

Eleven

BEN is in the shower. GEORGE has wine.

GEORGE: It's this city makes me act like a madwoman. I'd be different in another city. (*Pause.*) A holiday's the answer. Ben? The answer.

BEN: To what?

GEORGE: Everything.

BEN: Somewhere quiet.

GEORGE: I'm going to start over. I want a new job.

BEN: Eh?

GEORGE: A new job.

BEN: You've just got a new job.

GEORGE: I know but it's driving me crazy. That's why we keep fighting. It's my job that makes us fight. Something completely different. Something I know nothing about. I'm going to learn some languages. That's the future. I'm going to learn how to say 'hello, it's very pleasant to meet you' in ten different countries. I want to look different. I'm in a rut I think. We're both in a rut. All we need to do is change everything in our lives and everything'll be fine.

BEN: Eh?

GEORGE: Change. Change everything. You probably think you're happy with it all. But it's that kind of satisfaction that leads to complacency.

BEN: Don't drink all the wine.

GEORGE: I'm going to stop drinking completely. After tonight I won't drink another drop in my life.

BEN: Eh?

GEORGE: Never drink again. I'll be tee-total. I need things to be extreme! Don't you see?

BEN: Shall we open another?

GEORGE: Yeah. Finish it up. Then I can start afresh tomorrow.

GEORGE gets fully clothed into the shower with BEN.

BEN: George! What the hell are you – ?

Twelve

KATE: You're boiling. Are you boiling?

SARAH: No.

KATE: I'm sorry. It's the window. It's stuck.

SARAH: I'll look at it.

KATE: I'm really sorry.

SARAH: I'm fine, honestly.

KATE: You're boiling.

Pause.

SARAH picks up KATE's red dress. She holds it against herself.

SHARON picks up a dress, echoing this action, holds it against herself.

SARAH: (*Picking up KATE's dress.*) Put it on.

KATE: You'll laugh.

SARAH: I won't.

KATE puts on the red dress.

KATE: Well? Do I look like the devil incarnate?

SARAH: Do you want to?

KATE: Tell me I look foxy.

SARAH: You look really sweet.

KATE: Screw you!

SARAH: You look like…a red angel.

KATE: I'm gonna tout my wares on the street.

SARAH: You better watch yourself out there girl. It's a jungle out there.

KATE: Men'll pay thousands to kiss me on the lips.

SARAH: Never kiss on the lips girl, ain't I taught you nothing?

KATE: Don't I look a tiny bit like a whore?

SARAH: Sixty/forty girl. That's the deal. I got contacts.

KATE: Get your pimping ass out my flat!

SARAH: Your flat?

KATE: Our flat. What about this? Does this look sexy?

KATE slides her strap off her shoulder.

SARAH: Stop it Kate.

KATE: Or this?

Slides her skirt up her thigh.

SARAH: Stop it!

Pause.

You look lovely in it.

KATE: I look stupid.

SARAH: You look great, honestly.

KATE: Not like Sandra Dee on a hen night?

SARAH: No.

KATE: (*Sings.*) 'Look at me…' You want some more wine?

SARAH: Are you trying to get me drunk?

KATE: Uhuh.

They drink.

I like your hair. Looks different.

SARAH: God, I hate it.

KATE: It's pretty.

SARAH: I look like Stig of the Dump.

KATE: No.

KATE touches SARAH's hair.

Song: 'Zero.'

RICHARD: There's no-one here today cos' someone took the light away.

BEN: There's nothing in my heart, don't think I could even start to explain.

GEORGE: I can't stand the pain of losing something so
    much a part of me
    Though in reality you were hardly there in my heart.

RICHARD/GEORGE: You were everything
    Everything…

Thirteen

RICHARD and SHARON.

RICHARD: What did you do today?

SHARON: Nothing.

RICHARD: You stayed in all day?

SHARON: I looked after Luke for a while. Took him to the
    park.

RICHARD: Then what?

SHARON: Did some shopping.

RICHARD: Then what?

SHARON: Nothing!

RICHARD: Then what?

SHARON: Nothing!

RICHARD: Why didn't you work today?

SHARON: My day off. You knew that.

RICHARD: You didn't meet anyone.

SHARON: I picked up Luke.

RICHARD: And went where with him baby?

SHARON: To the park. What is this?

RICHARD: You look nice baby.

SHARON: Thought I'd dress up.

RICHARD: For me?

SHARON: Who else is here?

Pause.

RICHARD: Touch me.

SHARON touches him half-heartedly then drops her hand.

Touch me.

She lets him touch her.

Tell me what you'd like.

SHARON: Don't you know?

RICHARD touches her.

RICHARD: Touch me.

SHARON: I'm tired of – Tired.

RICHARD: Touch me.

KATE lets SARAH watch her undress.

Sex scene with SHARON and RICHARD. BEN appears as fantasy/paranoia figure for SHARON/RICHARD.

Music cue: 'Soft Mistake' (instrumental).

RICHARD/GEORGE: You were everything
Everything…

Fourteen

RICHARD looks at SHARON.

RICHARD: You smell different.
You smell the way you used to smell when we first met.
Your hair is different.
I don't know how.

Don't know about hair.
You smile to yourself.
Hum a tune as you wash up.
Never used to.
You've lost weight.
Why would you want to lose weight?
You get every Monday off work.
You don't call me every lunchtime anymore.
We negotiate round each other at breakfast.
I ask you what you're thinking
I ask you what you're thinking
You say, I'm tired. That's all, baby, that's all.
You lie different in bed.
Turned away.
You don't curl your arm round my waist.
You don't kiss me awake.
I ask you what you're thinking
I ask you what you're thinking
You say, I'm tired. I'm tired of... I'm tired baby, that's all.
I watch you when you don't know I'm watching you.
Follow you from work.
A glimpse of your life when you're not with me.
You're ordinary.
Extraordinary.
Asking myself.
How do I
Know if I
Know you at all.
Asking
How do I
Know if I
Know you at all.

Fifteen

LONER, BEN and GEORGE.

The LONER is standing in GEORGE and BEN's bedroom. GEORGE sits wet from the shower on the bed. BEN is under the bed looking for the bottle opener.

GEORGE: Give him that funny fish one!

BEN: The funny fish one doesn't open.

GEORGE: It does so!

LONER: I can come back another time.

GEORGE: Get him the swanky metal one then.

BEN: You threw the metal one out the window.

GEORGE: I did not! (*To LONER.*) He made me throw it out the window.

LONER: It doesn't really matter.

GEORGE: How the hell did we open the wine then eh? If I threw the opener out the window?

BEN: I borrowed one from next door.

GEORGE: Well. Lend him the one you borrowed.

BEN: Here mate.

GEORGE: (*To LONER.*) I'd just like to say that there was severe provocation involved when I accidentally dropped the opener out the window. And no one was underneath so there were no casualties.

BEN: You could have killed someone love.

GEORGE: My lover has no sense of theatre.

BEN: My lover has no sense of responsibility.

43

LONER: Well thanks very much…

GEORGE: No offence darling, but who are you?

LONER: I live upstairs.

GEORGE: I know you. You're the one who puts the rubbish out after the binmen have come.

LONER: Yeah.

GEORGE: Well it's pleasant to meet you.

LONER: It's very pleasant to meet you.

GEORGE: You live alone?

BEN: George! Don't be nosy.

GEORGE: I'm being interested.

LONER: I live alone. I've lived in this city all my life.

GEORGE: And what are your hopes and aspirations?

BEN: George.

LONER: I'm a motorbike courier.

GEORGE: Oh well never mind.

LONER: It's just until… I like it.

BEN: Must be interesting. You get to meet people. Keep fit.

GEORGE: Ben.

BEN: What?

GEORGE: You're being patronising.

LONER: Well. Nice to meet you.

GEORGE: Come for dinner.

LONER: Oh thanks.

GEORGE: We'll call round and invite you.

BEN: Only if you want to.

LONER: I'll bring it back.

GEORGE: Who the hell did you borrow it from?

BEN: The couple upstairs.

GEORGE: That pair of freaks.

BEN: George! (*To LONER.*) Sorry.

GEORGE: He's a dodgy one, if you ask me.

BEN: You know nothing about them.

GEORGE: She thinks she's something special. Turns her nose up at me when we're in the lift.

BEN: I think they're nice.

GEORGE: You think everyone's nice. Nice, nice, fucking nice. What happened to heroes? My lover has no sense of passion.

LONER: Cheers, anyway.

GEORGE: He's quite cute though. Don't you think? Benjie? Isn't he cute?

LONER: I should get back.

GEORGE: Do you have a name?

BEN: Now who's being patronising?

LONER: It's er…Richard.

GEORGE: Well, er Richard. Do call again.

BEN: You're drunk.

GEORGE: Am not drunk. Am I drunk?

LONER: I…

BEN: My lover has no sense of responsibility.

GEORGE: Isn't he a prude? You're a big fucking girl's blouse!

BEN: Enjoy your wine.

GEORGE: See you again.

LONER leaves.

GEORGE: I like you. Stay. Ben, get him to stay and talk to me. Go on.

BEN: No.

Sixteen

RICHARD and SHARON.

RICHARD pushes a huge box into SHARON's room.

SHARON: You're joking right?

RICHARD: Won't be for long.

SHARON: Fit a bloody horse in there.

RICHARD: Not a whole horse. The tail would stick out.

SHARON: Take it away.

RICHARD: I can't.

SHARON: You can't keep it here. How am I gonna watch the telly?

RICHARD: Just a few days. That's all I'm asking.

SHARON: It's in the way.

RICHARD: Please.

SHARON: What's in it?

RICHARD: Trust me.

SHARON: You'll have to do better than that.

RICHARD: Let me keep it here for a few days. And don't open it.

SHARON: Why can't I open it?

RICHARD: Because that'll spoil everything. Why would you want to open it?

SHARON: If you loved me you'd let me.

RICHARD: If you loved me you'd trust me.

SHARON: I want to see!

RICHARD: Promise me.

SHARON: I'll stub my bloody toe on it.

RICHARD: Just a few days.

SHARON: Richard!!

RICHARD: Please, baby, please…

SHARON: Just a few days.

RICHARD: And you won't open it.

SHARON: I won't open it.

Car alarm goes off. All look out.

Seventeen

The LONER is drinking and has a language tape playing.

The voice on the tape speaks in English and then repeats the phrase in Lithuanian. The LONER repeats the words in Lithuanian. At the end of the scene he begins to speak over the tape in English.

TAPE: (*Voice off, English.*) Hello. (*Voice off, Lithuanian.*) Hello.

LONER: (*Repeats in Lithuanian.*) Hello.

TAPE: (*Voice off, English.*) It's very pleasant to meet you. (*Voice off, Lithuanian.*) It's very pleasant to meet you.

LONER: (*Repeats in Lithuanian.*) It's great to meet you.

TAPE: (*Voice off, English.*) How do I get to the square? (*Voice off, Lithuanian.*) How do I get to the square?

LONER: (*Repeats in Lithuanian.*) How do I...

TAPE: (*Voice off, English.*) A kilo please! (*Voice off, Lithuanian.*) A kilo please!

LONER: (*Repeats in Lithuanian.*) A kilo...

TAPE: (*Voice off, English.*) I have three brothers and four sisters. (*Voice off, Lithuanian.*) I have three brothers and four sisters.

LONER: (*Repeats in Lithuanian.*) I have ten brothers and ten sisters.

TAPE: (*Voice off, English.*) My sister is ten years older than me. (*Voice off, Lithuanian.*) My sister is ten years older than me.

LONER: ...

TAPE: (*Voice off, English.*) It's pleasant to meet you. (*Voice off, Lithuanian.*) It's pleasant to meet you.

LONER: (*Over Lithuanian.*) I took some photos today.

TAPE: (*Voice off, English.*) My brother has been married five times. (*Voice off, Lithuanian.*) My brother has been married five times.

LONER: (*Over Lithuanian.*) Just people in the street.

TAPE: (*Voice off, English.*) My brother's wife's skirt is too short and her lips are too red. (*Voice off, Lithuanian.*) My brother's wife's skirt is too short and her lips are too red.

LONER: (*Over Lithuanian.*) A woman with plastic bags tied round her feet and her legs all swollen.

TAPE: (*Voice off, Lithuanian.*) Do you have that in my size?

LONER: (*Over Lithuanian.*) A kid with the oldest looking face you've ever seen.

TAPE: (*Voice off, English.*) A room for one please. (*Voice off, Lithuanian.*) A room for one please.

LONER: (*Over Lithuanian.*) A little kid with a middle-aged face.

TAPE: (*Voice off, English.*) I have four brothers and two sisters. (*Voice off, Lithuanian.*) I have four brothers and two sisters.

LONER: (*Over Lithuanian.*) A business woman sitting crosslegged on the floor of the train station.

TAPE: (*Voice off, English.*) My brother is taller than I am. (*Voice off, Lithuanian.*) My brother is taller than I am.

LONER: (*Over Lithuanian.*) An old woman in a feather boa and silver shoes.

TAPE: (*Voice off, English.*) My brother is richer than I am. (*Voice off, Lithuanian.*) My brother is richer than I am.

LONER: (*Over Lithuanian.*) It's not intruding.

TAPE: (*Voice off, English.*) Ladies like my brother more than they like me. (*Voice off, Lithuanian.*) Ladies like my brother more than they like me.

LONER: (*Over Lithuanian.*) It's collecting.

TAPE: (*Voice off, English.*) It's very pleasant to meet you. (*Voice off, Lithuanian.*) It's very pleasant to meet you.

LONER: (*Over Lithuanian.*) It's great to meet you.

TAPE: (*Voice off, English.*) A room for one please! (*Voice off, Lithuanian.*) A room for one please!

LONER: (*Repeats in Lithuanian.*) A room for one please!

TAPE: (*Voice off, English.*) I live alone. (*Voice off, Lithuanian.*) I live alone.

LONER: (*Repeats in Lithuanian.*) I live alone.

KATE appears at the LONER's door.

LONER is trying to turn the language tape off; it starts bleating away in the background.

TAPE: (*Voice off, English.*) I have three brothers and two sisters. (*Voice off, Lithuanian.*) I have three brothers and two sisters. (*Voice off, English.*) My brother's wife wears her skirts too short and her lipsticks too red. (*Voice off, Lithuanian.*) My brother's wife wears her skirts too short and her lipsticks too red. (*Voice off, English.*) I'll have a room for one. (*Voice off, Lithuanian.*) I'll have a room for one. (*Voice off, English.*) A room for one. (*Voice off, Lithuanian.*) A room for one. (*Voice off, English.*) A room for one please. (*Voice off, Lithuanian.*) A room for one please. (*Voice off, English.*) I live alone. (*Voice off, Lithuanian.*) I live alone. (*Voice off, English.*) It's great to meet you!

He manages to turn it off.

LONER: Sorry.

KATE: I'm Kate.

LONER: Hi Kate.

KATE: What was that?

LONER: Conversational Lithuanian.

KATE: What are you learning that for?

LONER: For a laugh.

KATE looks at the LONER's anti-gravity boots.

KATE: I like what you've done with this place. Never see you do we? Keep yourself to yourself.

LONER: I don't mean to.

KATE: Feel like you're scared of me.

LONER: I...

KATE: When I say hello. Rabbit in the headlights.

LONER: I'm not good at –

KATE: Forming sentences?

LONER: I don't mean to be rude but –

KATE: I wondered about you.

LONER: Why?

KATE: My mystery neighbour. (*Beat.*) The girl opposite thinks you're a serial killer.

LONER: Sorry?

KATE: That's what she told me.

LONER: The girl opposite? The couple?

KATE: Yeah. Some of my post went astray. When she brought it round a few weeks back she told me to be careful coming home at night.

LONER: Why would she think that about me?

KATE: She said quiet ones are the worst.

Pause.

I came to borrow a bottle opener.

LONER: Oh.

KATE: Is that alright?

LONER: Of course. I'll just find it.

Goes to look. Stops.

What had I done to make her think I was a serial killer?

KATE shrugs.

LONER thinks about this. Disturbed by the thought.

Sorry, what was I saying?

KATE: You were looking for the opener.

LONER: The opener?

KATE: The bottle opener.

LONER: Ah, yeah, I'll – Yes –

KATE: You know how it is.

LONER: It's around here somewhere.

KATE: The bottle opener bermuda triangle.

LONER: I just used it.

KATE: I lose things all the time.

LONER: I never usually lose anything.

Pause.

LONER finds the opener and gives it to KATE.

So I hadn't done anything in particular to make her think I was a serial killer?

KATE: I shouldn't have said anything.

LONER: It's okay.

KATE: I sometimes just say whatever comes into my head. Sarah's always saying I should be more careful.

LONER: Who's Sarah?

KATE: My new flatmate. My friend. Well. Thanks.

LONER: (*Suddenly.*) Would you like a drink?

KATE: Oh. Well. I would but.

LONER: Doesn't matter.

KATE: It's just. Sarah's just moved in. We were going to celebrate.

LONER: Forget it. Honestly.

KATE: And I could ask you round. But Sarah.

LONER: It's fine.

KATE: Doesn't always. Like. Unexpected. Company.

LONER: Another time.

KATE: Well thanks for this.

LONER: No problem.

KATE: I'll bring it back.

Eighteen

BEN and GEORGE.

GEORGE: Stop it.

BEN: Stop what?

GEORGE: Doing that with your face.

BEN: Everything I do pisses you off.

GEORGE: Not everything.

Pause.

I didn't want to come home.

BEN: The party was over.

GEORGE: It wasn't over.

BEN: It was over as soon as you called Jennifer a milch cow.

GEORGE: She took it the wrong way.

BEN: It was a chilled party. A mellow party.

GEORGE: I was shaking things up a bit.

BEN: Sometimes things don't have to be shaken. Sometimes, things are fine as they are.

GEORGE: Nothing's fine. I'm not happy. Not with anything.

BEN: I know that.

GEORGE: So do something about it. Make me feel how I used to for Christ sake! We used to feel special. We used to feel young.

BEN: I don't know what you want. I don't know what to give you.

GEORGE: Stop that.

BEN: Stop what.

GEORGE: Looking at me like that!

BEN: I'm not looking at you like anything.

GEORGE: I didn't want to come home.

BEN: The party was over.

GEORGE: You always have to be the fucking wet blanket don't you? Telling it like it is.

BEN: It was over.

GEORGE: Maybe I don't want you to tell it like it is. Maybe I want to think the party's still going.

BEN: I'm going to bed.

GEORGE: Don't fucking turn your back on me!

BEN: I don't know what you want anymore! I don't know what to say!

GEORGE: Say what'll make me happy. Say what I want to hear. Say something nice.

BEN: I do love you.

Pause.

GEORGE: I don't believe you.

Nineteen

SHARON is struggling not to open box.

Song: 'Bonfire'.

SHARON: Have you ever wondered why those days exist
When life just seems to be a conspiracy against you
I don't know where the answers lie
But I try not to get hung up on the questions

I burn like a good bonfire, in whatever I do
Burn like a good bonfire and I know I'll pull through
The time is long overdue for a house clearing of the soul
We all get so complicated in our lives

SHARON/GEORGE: We walk and just walk, sit and just sit, we be and just be

SHARON: Above all don't stray from your chosen path
Burn like a good bonfire, in whatever you do
Burn like a good bonfire, and I know you'll pull through
Burn like a good bonfire, in whatever you do
Burn like a good bonfire, may peace come to you

ALL: The time is long overdue for a house-clearing of the
soul
We all get so complicated in our lives

Burn like a good bonfire, in whatever you do
Burn like a good bonfire, and I know you'll pull through
Burn like a good bonfire, in whatever you do
Burn like a good bonfire, may peace come to you

Twenty

KATE and SARAH.

KATE: What does she look like?

SARAH: Who?

KATE: His new woman.

SARAH: I told you, she doesn't matter.

KATE: Is she pretty?

SARAH: She's history.

KATE: He told you that?

SARAH: As good as.

KATE: Has she got big tits?

SARAH: Why?

KATE: I want to square up to the competition.

SARAH: She's nothing on you.

KATE: What should I do then?

SARAH: You want my advice?

KATE: I always need your advice! You think I should say something.

SARAH: Not yet. Let things grow a bit. I think you should give it time.

KATE: But what if I'm wasting my time?

SARAH: Something will happen.

KATE: You sure?

SARAH: Maybe just not what you expect.

KATE: Do you think we'd be suited?

SARAH: You get on with me don't you?

KATE: What would he like about me?

SARAH: Everything.

KATE: Tell me. Tell me.

SARAH: He'd like your laugh. It makes you shake all over. Makes other people want to laugh too.

KATE: Really?

SARAH: He'd like your mind. The way you look at things.

KATE: How do I look at things?

SARAH: Differently.

KATE: He'd like your smile. Open. Welcomes people in. He'd like your eyes. Bright. Intelligent. The colour of them. He'd like your body. He'd want to touch you but he wouldn't dare.

KATE: Maybe I'd let him.

SARAH: Would you?

KATE: Yeah I'd let him. Let him run his fingers down my spine.

SARAH: He'd like that.

KATE: I'd be too afraid to say. To ask him.

SARAH: You shouldn't ever be afraid.

KATE: I'd dither. Not get on with it.

SARAH: You will. When you feel safe enough. Confident enough.

Pause.

Listen Kate. I've got something to tell you.

KATE: What?

SARAH: He's coming round to dinner with us. Tomorrow.

KATE: Tomorrow?

SARAH: You pleased?

KATE: I won't know what to say.

SARAH: You can talk more easily. With me there.

KATE: Yeah, you'll have to be there.

SARAH: And when you've broken the ice, I can leave you alone.

KATE: (*Hugging her.*) You're the best Sarah, the best!

Twenty-one

BEN sleeps.

GEORGE: I love you when you're asleep
You look like a kid who's found his toy
We don't itch and scratch at each other
I love you when you're asleep
Just goes to fuck when you open your eyes.

Cut to LONER speaking Lithuanian.

Song: 'Feela'.

You saw me crying, but you didn't want to look
You heard me hurting, but you didn't want to listen

GEORGE/BEN: This could have been something
This could have been really something
Tell me something more
Tell me something more worth living for

GEORGE: You felt me wanting but you didn't want to give
You sensed me sinking but you really couldn't save me

GEORGE/KATE: This could have been something
  This could have been really something
  Tell me something more
  Tell me something more worth living for

KATE/LONER: This could have been something
  This could have been really something
  Tell me something more
  Tell me something more worth living for

Car alarm goes off.

Twenty-two

SARAH and RICHARD meet.

SARAH: Do you know whose car that is?

RICHARD: What?

SARAH: The car. I want to switch off that bloody alarm.

RICHARD: Oh. I don't know.

SARAH: I've just moved in with Kate. Well, I'm her flatmate. You know.

RICHARD: Oh right.

SARAH: You live here.

RICHARD: No. Well. Why?

SARAH: I just – wondered –

RICHARD: I mean. I'm here a lot. But this isn't my permanent address.

SARAH: Right. I'm Sarah.

RICHARD: Right.

SARAH: I didn't catch your name.

RICHARD: Yeah. You seen that moon tonight?

SARAH: The moon?

RICHARD: It's amazing. A full moon. Weird shit happens when there's a full moon.

SARAH: We all turn into werewolves you mean?

RICHARD: Yeah, could be. Imagine. That'd be wicked!

SARAH: You live in there?

RICHARD: I don't – Sharon lives there. This isn't my permanent – Look –

SARAH: Sharon's the one with the amazing voice.

RICHARD: Eh?

SARAH: Your girlfriend. I heard her singing.

RICHARD: No. That wouldn't be her.

SARAH: I thought it was coming from there. Beautiful.

RICHARD: Sharon doesn't sing.

SARAH: I'd best be getting back.

RICHARD: Yeah. What was your name again?

SARAH: Sarah.

RICHARD nods and leaves.

Twenty-three

LONER and KATE sing together to music KATE is listening to.

LONER exercises in his room.

Twenty-four

GEORGE and BEN.

GEORGE: You want to know why I got drunk? Because I came downstairs when you were talking to Sam in the kitchen. And you were moving round her fixing yourself a drink. And Jennifer was making one of her speeches about porn being the highest form of feminism and you and Sam didn't even bother to put her right. And when Jennifer took a drink you and Sam just looked at each other.

BEN: I've known Sam since we were –

GEORGE: I'm not jealous of her. I'm not. But I almost didn't recognise you. I watched you and Sam from the doorway, this silent communication of glances and gestures. The way you two can share a thought without saying a word. And I knew I'd never seen you be that free with me.

Pause.

BEN: I don't know what to say.

Twenty-five

KATE and SARAH.

SARAH: When you get together. I'll miss talking to you.

KATE: We'll still talk.

SARAH: Maybe he'll be jealous.

KATE: No. He wouldn't.

SARAH: But I'd have known you longer.

KATE: He wouldn't mind.

SARAH: What if he made you choose. Me or him. What would you say?

KATE: He wouldn't make me choose.

SARAH: He might. You don't know him like I do. You have to tell him how you feel Kate. You have to.

KATE: You said it was too soon.

SARAH: I've changed my mind. You can't keep wondering forever. Can you?

KATE: I'm scared.

SARAH: Tell him tomorrow Kate. I'll help you.

Twenty-six

LONER with the language tape.

TAPE: (*Voice off, English.*) Hello. (*Voice off, Lithuanian.*) Hello.

LONER: (*Lithuanian.*) Hello.

TAPE: (*Voice off, English.*) It's pleasant to meet you. (*Voice off, Lithuanian.*) It's pleasant to meet you.

LONER: (*Lithuanian.*) It's pleasant to meet you.

TAPE: (*Voice off, English.*) Your eyes are the colour of sunsets. (*Voice off, Lithuanian.*) Your eyes are the colour of sunsets.

LONER: (*Over Lithuanian.*) Yeah.

TAPE: (*Voice off, English.*) Your smile burns like a bonfire. (*Voice off, Lithuanian.*) Your smile burns like a bonfire.

LONER: (*Lithuanian.*) …

TAPE: (*Voice off, English.*) Your hands are gentle. (*Voice off, Lithuanian.*) Your hands are gentle.

LONER: (*Lithuanian.*) …

TAPE: (*Voice off, English.*) Your voice is sweet. (*Voice off, Lithuanian.*) Your voice is sweet.

LONER: (*Over Lithuanian.*) You say whatever comes into your head.

TAPE: (*Voice off, English.*) Hello. (*Voice off, Lithuanian.*) Hello.

LONER: (*Lithuanian.*) Hello

TAPE: (*Voice off, English.*) It's pleasant to meet you. (*Voice off, Lithuanian.*) It's pleasant to meet you.

LONER: (*Lithuanian.*) It's great to meet you. Come round again.

TAPE: (*Voice off, English.*) I want you to make love to me, Richard. (*Voice off, Lithuanian.*) I want you to make love to me, Richard.

LONER: (*Over Lithuanian.*) Okay.

TAPE: (*Voice off, English.*) You know you want to, Richard, all you have to do is believe… (*Voice off, Lithuanian.*) You know you want to, Richard, all you have to do is believe…

LONER: (*Over Lithuanian.*) …

TAPE: (*Voice off, English.*) A room for one please! (*Voice off, Lithuanian.*) A room for one please!

LONER: (*Over Lithuanian.*) …

TAPE: (*Voice off, English.*) Talk to her, Richard. (*Voice off, Lithuanian.*) Talk to her, Richard. (*Voice off, English.*) Talk to her, Richard. (*Voice off, Lithuanian.*) Talk to her, Richard. (*Voice off, English.*) Let her understand you, Richard! (*Voice off, Lithuanian.*) Let her understand you, Richard!

Twenty-seven

SARAH is listening to a walkman. The beat starts to be heard by the other characters and they react to it.

SHARON opens the crate. Contents spills out and fills room.

SHARON panicks at first trying frantically to push contents back into box. Then she becomes resigned, almost relieved that this may be a sign that can end the relationship for them.

RICHARD returns and finds her with crate contents. They look at each other.

Twenty-eight

LONER and KATE.

KATE: Hi.

LONER: Oh. Hi.

KATE: What are you doing?

LONER: I like taking pictures of people when they don't know I am.

KATE: Isn't that a bit creepy?

LONER: I suppose.

KATE: Serial killers always have loads of pictures of their victims on their walls.

LONER: Do they?

KATE: They do in films.

LONER: Oh.

Pause.

KATE: Will you take one of me?

LONER: Okay.

He stops.

I can't.

KATE: What?

LONER: I can't do it with you watching me.

KATE: What?

Pause.

I brought back the bottle opener.

LONER: You've finished with it?

KATE: I think I've had enough.

LONER: Very sensible.

KATE: I'm not trying to be sensible. I don't mean to…

LONER: I just meant…

KATE: I know. It's okay. Do you take pictures of me when I'm not watching?

LONER: No. I've never taken pictures of you.

KATE: But you might?

LONER: I take pictures of the street. And whoever's in it.

KATE: I like it. Creepy. But I like it.

Beat. SARAH enters. Watches them.

Dance with me.

LONER: Dance with you?

KATE: Yeah.

LONER: Why?

KATE: 'Cos I'm drunk. 'Cos I'm fearless.

She starts to dance.

You're okay aren't you?

LONER: Am I?

KATE: Yeah. I don't think you could be a serial killer.

LONER: Thanks.

KATE notices SARAH. KATE stops dancing.

SARAH: What's going on? What are you doing?

Pause.

What are you doing to her?

KATE: Sarah.

LONER: Nothing. I wasn't doing anything.

KATE: I was dancing.

SARAH: She's drunk.

LONER: I'm sorry. What is it you want? She came to –

SARAH: You can't just walk into a stranger's bedroom, the state you're in.

KATE: I was dancing.

SARAH: You better not hurt her.

SARAH sees the photos on the wall.

What's this?

LONER: They're mine. I take them. People in the street. I like the way they – they don't know they're being watched. I like the way people behave when they think they're alone. It's just photographs – it's not anything –

SARAH: Shut it, pervy bastard. You're drunk Kate. And people like him just want to take advantage of that.

LONER: I – I don't know what you think but you are –

SARAH: Get out.

LONER: Completely out of –

SARAH: Get out. Get out!

The LONER leaves his flat. SARAH and KATE look at each other.

What the hell are you doing? A middle-class Princess like you making out she could cut it as a whore. You don't even know him. What he's capable of. And you can't go round throwing yourself at people like a stupid little tart just 'cos you've got something to prove.

KATE: This is fucked up.

Twenty-nine

GEORGE and BEN.

GEORGE: Don't look at me like that.

BEN: How am I looking at you?

GEORGE: I'm tired. Of feeling I do everything wrong.

BEN: Everything I do pisses you off.

GEORGE: Not everything. The way you looked at me tonight.

BEN: I don't like you when you're drunk.

GEORGE: Maybe you don't like me full stop. You think I'm a slutty old alcoholic.

BEN: George…

GEORGE: Just hit me. Go on. Slap me across the face. It's what you're itching to do every time we go out.

BEN: You think I'd hit you.

GEORGE: Go on then.

BEN: You think I'd hit you.

GEORGE: It's you makes me drink. The way you give me that smug look, like darling you've had enough. It makes me rebel. It makes me get totally off my tits just to see what you'll do.

BEN: You didn't have to come home.

GEORGE: That emotional blackmail bullshit. That hangdog look you give everyone, so they go, poor little Ben, stuck with the silly drunk slag.

BEN: Nobody says that.

GEORGE: Your looks and glances. The way you correct me. The way you're smug and have to be right.

BEN: I don't have to be –

GEORGE: So leave! It's what you want! Bloody leave!

BEN: You bloody leave!

GEORGE: Everything is wrong! It's all wrong! It's all fucked! And you won't even see it! You won't even let anything change!

She starts to try to hit his chest and he grabs her wrists. This becomes a physical struggle.

Thirty

SHARON sings 'Gabriel', while thinking about BEN.

SHARON: I can fly
    But I want his wings
    I can shine even in the darkness
    But I crave the light that he brings
    Revel in the songs that he sings
    My angel Gabriel
    I can love
    But I need his heart
    I am strong even in my own
    But from him I never want to part
    He's been there since the very start
    My angel Gabriel
    My angel Gabriel
    Bless the day he came to be
    Angel's wings carried him to me
    Heavenly
    I can fly
    But I want his wings
    I can shine even in the darkness
    But I crave the light that he brings
    Revel in the songs that he sings
    My angel Gabriel
    My angel Gabriel
    My angel Gabriel

Car alarm goes off. All look out.

Thirty-one

BEN and GEORGE are making the bed after the fight. GEORGE won't look at him.

BEN: I'm sorry.
   We can't do this anymore.
   Can we?
   George?
   Everything I say irritates you.
   Every conversation becomes a fight.
   George?
   I don't know what to do.
   I don't know what to do.

Thirty-two

KATE and SARAH.

KATE: What the hell's got into you?
   We were talking.
   Say something for fuck's sake.

SARAH: I lost it.

KATE: I don't even know you. Do I? We don't even know
   each other at all.

SARAH: I was jealous.

KATE: I'm going out.

SARAH: Kate –

   Pause.

KATE: I don't understand.

SARAH: You do understand.

   SARAH tries to touch KATE.

KATE: Get off me! Just fucking get off!

Thirty-three

RICHARD and SHARON.

SHARON: Stop moving about, what's got into you?

RICHARD: Nothing baby

SHARON: Who're you phoning at this time of night?

RICHARD: No one baby, I just got to –

SHARON: I just want a conversation – all day at work it's like I'm invisible. It's like no one's gonna stop and ask my opinion. Nobody thinks my opinion's worth anything.

RICHARD: I know baby.

SHARON: Sometimes what I think is worth hearing. Sometimes –

RICHARD: I know baby. I just got a lot on my mind. But I'll get this payoff soon baby and then everyone's gonna listen to us. You'll see. Everybody'll hang on your every word then.

Thirty-four

BEN and GEORGE.

Pause.

GEORGE: Don't leave me.

Thirty-five

LONER loses it with the incessant language tape bleating. He pulls at the tape.

He picks up the mobile.

TAPE: (*Voice off, Lithuanian.*) Hello.

LONER: (*Over Lithuanian.*) It's me.

TAPE: (*Voice off, Lithuanian.*) Hello!

LONER: (*Over Lithuanian.*) I know you won't get this.

TAPE: (*Voice off, English.*) It's pleasant to meet you! (*Voice off, Lithuanian.*) It's pleasant to meet you!

LONER: (*Over Lithuanian.*) But call me if you do.

TAPE: (*Voice off, Lithuanian.*) Hello!

Tape gets stuck.

LONER: I don't even know where in the hell you are.

TAPE: (*Voice off, Lithuanian.*) Hello! Hello!

LONER: I don't mind being alone.

TAPE: (*Voice off, Lithuanian.*) Hello! Hello! Hello!

LONER: I just wanted to hear your voice. I just wanted to hear your voice.

Thirty-six

BEN and SHARON meet in the lift.

SHARON touches the necklace. They look at each other. The necklace breaks.

SHARON: It's not my fault.
   It's the way he has to be the last to leave
   Can't be the first to speak
   It's not me
   It's the way he talks to drunks on park benches
   Never pays for his mistakes
   And every gift is never just a gift.
   It's not my fault
   He makes my mind stray

He makes my eyes wander
It's him
It's the way we kiss and all I can taste is the
disappointment.
But when we meet in the street. I know.
You can sense it too.
You're meant to be with me.
You're meant to be with me.

They kiss. Lift doors close.

Thirty-seven

SARAH and KATE.

SARAH: I shouldn't have moved in. Should I?

Pause.

I had to say Kate. Sometimes you just have to tell the truth.

KATE: Sometimes it's better if you don't.

SARAH: Touch me.

KATE: Leave me alone.

SARAH: Touch me.

Pause.

What is it that you want? You were playing with me.

KATE: He's not coming round here is he?

SARAH: No.

KATE: He doesn't even know I'm alive does he?

SARAH: No. (*Pause.*) I love you.

Lift doors open. BEN and SHARON stand apart looking out. We see that the moment earlier did not happen.

Thirty-eight

RICHARD and SHARON.

RICHARD: I know you say you don't need things baby, that you're happy living on nothing, but I'm gonna have you live like a princess, you'll see. You'll have more than you could ever need. Anything you want baby. I'll buy it for you.

SHARON: I want to do that course. I want to get my brain working again. Feel like I'm achieving something.

RICHARD: Just give me time, baby. I'll buy you any course you want. Just see. You'll see baby. You'll see.

Thirty-nine

SARAH and KATE. KATE is packing.

SARAH: I thought it was what you wanted to hear. What are you doing?

KATE: Why did you have to say anything?

SARAH: You have to say something. So someone knows who you are. You need someone to know who you are. You knew.

KATE: No

SARAH: You knew.

KATE finishes packing.

Don't go. You're scared.

Forty

RICHARD and SHARON.

RICHARD is on his mobile. He finishes the call.

RICHARD: What?

SHARON: If you weren't such a lousy liar it'd be funny.

RICHARD: What d'you mean?

SHARON: Can you believe I used to find it sexy? What does that say about me eh? Something illicit about you. That cocky Del-boy chat you gave me. Made me laugh. Thought I'd sort you out. How stupid's that eh? Maybe I'm getting old baby.

Cut to LONER.

LONER: I want us to talk properly.

Cut back to SHARON and RICHARD.

SHARON: I want us to tell the truth.

RICHARD: I do baby.

Pause.

What have you got to tell me?

SHARON: What?

RICHARD: You gonna be honest at last?

SHARON: About what?

RICHARD: Him.

SHARON: Who?

RICHARD: Tell me who he is.

SHARON: I don't know what you –

RICHARD: Tell me who he is.

SHARON: Richard…

RICHARD: Don't start that. You want honesty? You start then. Tell me who he is.

SHARON: Who?

RICHARD: Him. The guy you meet. Fuck. Talk to. Whatever it is you do.

SHARON: There's no one else!

RICHARD: Don't lie to me! I'll forgive you baby. But you got to tell me who he is.

SHARON: I swear.

RICHARD: When is this gonna stop eh? You're killing me here. Killing me.

SHARON: Touch me.

Pause.

Touch me baby.

Pause.

Why can't you trust me? I don't understand!

RICHARD: You do understand! Get off me! Just fucking get off!

Forty-one

BEN and GEORGE.

GEORGE: It's not about whether you love me.

Pause.

See you around.

Neither of them move.

Forty-two

RICHARD and SHARON. SHARON leaves during his speech.

RICHARD: It's all gonna take off like a rocket. Come right. You just needed a bit more faith. That's all. I just needed you to wait a little longer. I'm gonna come round here with so many gifts you'll be buried under them. I'll be doing some job that makes you proud. Makes me proud. I'll be proving all those fuckers wrong down through the years. I won't be the clown. The joker. Moon boy. I'll be made of something. You'll look up to me baby. Anything you want I'll click my fingers and make it yours. You just had to wait a little bit longer. That's all.

Song: 'Just Is'.

GEORGE: What kind of fool am I
    Reaching into a world I thought had changed
    Somehow rearranged

SARAH: Here I am
    Stepping into the night
    Like a keenly sharpened knife
    Carving holes in my life
    When I know that…

ALL: What is, just is
    What is, just is

GEORGE: You see I've been somewhere
    Not far away but such a different place
    Just to sit in one place

SHARON: And just when I thought I could take no more
    The bells started to ring
    And my soul to sing
    And I know that…

ALL: What is, just is
    What is, just is
    Chasing the tail of understanding as it runs through my life

RICHARD kicks hell out of the box.

GEORGE is alone.

SARAH comes looking for bottle opener.

LONER comes with bottle opener.

BEN comes looking for bottle opener from one of them.

Brief meeting of group.

KATE returns to SARAH. Puts her suitcase down.

Car is stolen outside.

Forty-three

LONER's mobile rings. For a moment he is amazed it is ringing. Then he answers.

LONER: Hello?

It's – it's great to – to speak to you.
Where are you?
What language do they speak there?

There is a noise from one of the other flats: RICHARD kicking hell out of the crate.

What? It was nothing. One of the neighbours. I'm here on my own.
Not lonely.
I want you to be happy too.
It's great.
But you are –
You are – Looking after yourself?
I know it's not safe.
I don't know how to deal with the idea you're not safe.
I don't know what I mean.
I know you can't come back yet.
I'm not waiting.

Pause.

Me too.

LONER closes the curtains on his room.